FINDING YOURSELF IN SCRIPTURE

D1316284

Cover design by Carlos Weaver.
Copy editing by Rori Madril, Lisa Garcia, and Danielle Rzepka.

ISBN: 978-0-9802362-2-4

Published by Life Teen, Inc.
2222 S. Dobson Rd.
Suite 601
Mesa, AZ 85202
www.lifeteen.com

Printed in the United States of America.
Printed on acid-free paper.

For more information about Life Teen or to order additional copies, go online to www.lifeteen.com or call us at 1-800-809-3902.

DEDICATION

To the students, staff and faculty at St. Timothy's Catholic school, and especially to all of the middle school youth I've prayed and journeyed with over these past several years.

The Lord has blessed me tremendously through all of you. Your desire to know the Lord, your hunger for and openness to His Word and your quest for holiness leave me speechless.

Thank you for how you love Jesus.

Continue to walk with Him daily and allow His Word to illuminate your path (Psalm 119:105).

Always remember how good you are!

FINDING YOURSELF IN SCRIPTURE

INTRODUCTION

THERE are a lot of ways that you can
get to know someone: you can hear about them from other people,
you can check out their MySpace or Facebook profiles, or you can
watch how they interact with others. If they're famous, you might
even catch an interview or read a book about their life. None of these
methods, though, are nearly as effective as sitting with that person,
one on one, and asking them meaningful questions like:

How does it make you feel when...?
Where did you grow up and what was your childhood like?
What are you most afraid of?
When do you feel the most joy?
Why do you do what you do?
Who is your personal hero?
What roles do God and faith play in your life?

Questions like these help you to get past the shallow things we
usually talk about, helping you to *really know a person.* They reveal
a person's true identity. While you can use these questions to get to
know other people, they are also a great starting point for getting to
know yourself. Where does your identity come from? Where do your
beliefs come from? What (or who) do you base your decisions on?
These are all important questions to reflect on and they should all
lead you back to one fundamental truth: **God is the author of your
life.**

That's right, God is the author and you are the character in His story,
not the other way around. God created you. He loves you and wants
you here. God has a plan for you. And if you *really want to know
yourself,* the best and fastest way to do that is to get to know the One
who created you.

The Bible is a great way to get to know the Author of your story. By reading about His interactions with other characters, specifically young Bible characters, you can get to know not only how God thinks and moves, but how others have responded to Him in both right and wrong ways.

When you read Scripture, you will see that while customs and traditions change, people really don't change all that much. You'll realize that you have more in common with Biblical characters than you would have originally thought. We aren't just reading about people from thousands of years ago. No, when we read the Bible it's like we're reading about ourselves. God doesn't change. So knowing what did and did not please God in other people is a great way of knowing what does and does not please God in us.

In this book you are going to be reintroduced to ten young Bible characters and their stories. Some you might know well. Others you might not recognize at all. Some are heroic. Some are heart breaking. But they're all thoroughly human. If you look hard enough, you might find a little bit of yourself in each story. At the very least, you'll be given an introduction to a God who is madly in love with you.

It's important to remember that while God might not love everything you do, **He does love you.** And, He is cheering you on to sainthood. This book will act as a small step in that direction. Some of these characters' lives will make you feel quite holy. Others will teach you how to become even holier. In the pages that follow, you'll be guided and invited to open the Bible for yourself and read parts of their story again.

These people all have something worth imitating and something worth following. Learn from them. What you'll soon realize is that living as a Christian is not so much about "finding yourself" as it is about finding and unleashing Christ's presence and power within yourself. The more you recognize God's presence in you, your home, your school, the Church, and the world, the better you'll be able to share God's love with all you come into contact with.

The secret to a joyful life and a hope-filled future isn't about figuring out tomorrow; it's about listening to God *today*. God, the Author of Life, has something to say to you through the brothers and sisters who came before you. If you want to know God better, just take a deep breath and turn the page.

It's story time.

x

ABEL
THE BIBLE'S FIRST "LITTLE BROTHER"

NO FAMILY is perfect. The Holy Family, consisting of our Lord Jesus, our Blessed Mother Mary, and St. Joseph, is as close as you get. Even the Holy Family wasn't perfect. But oh, so close!

Every family is imperfect. Some families are holy and some are not. Some families are huge, while others are small. Some families are financially well-off and others struggle to pay the bills. Every family is unique in their struggles and in their blessings. Yet, they all have one thing in common: every family, absolutely every family, is imperfect. Those families you see on television, in magazine ads, or on billboards all appear to be perfect in every way. But, you guessed it, they're imperfect, too.

Now, some families are a little easier to grow up in than others, but every family has their challenges. I'll use my family as an example. I come from a family of six kids. On the surface it sounds great. There were always people around. The house was busy and loud, and holidays were outrageous.

I was child number five. The four children ahead of me were *perfect*, or at least they seemed that way. They aced every class they took and they were the captains of their respective sports teams. In everything they did, they were the best. It wasn't enough that they played an instrument, they had to sit first chair in band. It wasn't enough that they'd get a part in the play, they always had to get the lead part in the play. You get the idea.

As if that wasn't enough pressure, along came one more child after me: my baby brother. He stole all the attention and had absolute parental protection. Everything he did was cute and amazing in everyone's eyes. Suddenly, I felt like nothing I did was good enough. When measured up to my siblings' accomplishments, I felt like a nothing. I became bitter and annoyed. What made everyone else so special?

I felt a lot like the famous Biblical character named Cain, who comes onto the scene very early in Scripture. Cain was Adam and Eve's first-born son after they were thrown out of Eden. He was the only son until, one day, he had a "perfect" younger brother of his own.

Whether you're an older or younger sibling, or an only child, the story of the sibling rivalry between Cain and Abel has elements that we can all relate to. Take a minute, now, and read the story yourself: **Genesis 4:1-12**.

GIVING GOD YOUR BEST
—WHAT'S RIGHT, NOT WHAT'S LEFT

Cain means "spear."

Cain and Abel's story is famous in Scripture. Did it leave you confused? It's pretty quick and, if you don't know what to look for, you might have missed why it was such a big deal to God.

It starts out simple enough, right? Adam and Eve have two sons, Cain and Abel. Together, it's as though the family works on a farm: Cain tends to the crops while Abel tends to the animals. At this point, they decide to make a sacrifice to God.

Abel means "breath."

Cain and Abel both offer a sacrifice to God, but God's reaction isn't the same to each brother. However, a clue is hidden in verses four and five as to why God likes Abel's sacrifice so much more than his older brother's. Take another look:

"...and Abel brought of the firstlings of his flock and of their fat portions. And the Lord had regard for Abel and his offering, but for Cain and his offering he had no regard. So Cain was very angry..."
– Genesis 4:4-5

Many people read over this passage and think that it only has to do with the sacrifice. You see, Abel gave God the best animal(s) that he had. The word "firstling" means the first crop or first animal of a season, which also means the *best* crop or *best* animal of that season. The Scripture verse does not make a distinction like that about Cain's fruit offering. It's as if Abel went out into the herd of animals and found the absolute best to sacrifice, but Cain just grabbed whatever fruit was lying around (possibly bruised or rotting) and let that be his sacrifice. Imagine how good Abel's sacrifice must have been for such a distinction. I mean, that must have been some really good meat to make God so pleased, huh? It must have been the biggest, fattest, juiciest Grade A steak this world has ever seen for God to be so wowed by Abel's sacrifice, right?

Well, not exactly.

Yes, it does say that the offering was Abel's best, the prime choice; but what pleased God wasn't so much Abel's animal(s), but Abel's *attitude*. Notice that the verse says, *"but for Cain and his offering* he (God) had no regard." So it wasn't necessarily the crop that God was displeased with. God was displeased with Cain; something was wrong with Cain's attitude or with Cain's heart.

God even gives Cain another chance, explaining that if he offered a better sacrifice, he too would be held in high regard (Gen 4:7). Before we move on, though, it's important to note something here: God's love for Cain was not based on his performance. God's love is not about "what you do"; He loves you for who you are. Cain's lackluster sacrifice didn't mean that God loved Cain less, it meant that God was disappointed because Cain didn't love God more. He wanted to help Cain understand what true love requires; true love requires sacrifice. When we sacrifice, we show our love by putting others before ourselves.

You read how the story turned out. Cain was so jealous that he lashed out against his brother. He allowed his jealousy and anger to explode. Cain didn't just ignore Abel or punch him or break Eve's favorite vase and blame it on him. No, Cain killed his brother. The black sheep killed the white sheep, so to speak, and God was furious. Cain is then sent off alone. He got what he wanted. He wanted to put himself first and not have to "keep up" with his younger brother anymore. So there Cain went, alone, ashamed and awfully miserable.

But wait, this is supposed to be a chapter about Abel, right? So let's take a look at the hero/victim of the story – the Bible's first "little brother," Abel.

FINDING YOUR STORY IN ABEL'S STORY

Have you ever felt "competitive" with a brother or sister?

Do you hold anything back from God or do you give Him your best, every day?

Do you worry more about what others think or what God thinks?

Have you ever wondered why we "sacrifice" things to God, anyway? Have you ever asked why God wanted us to sacrifice to Him? What do you think?

A. Does God hate animals or something?
B. Is He a strict vegetarian?
C. Is God just bloodthirsty?
D. Or is it something bigger?

The answer is D: something bigger. Since God is the Creator of all things, it means that *absolutely every thing* is a gift from the Creator: every drop of rain, blade of grass, piece of fruit, animal and person.

When God asks us, His creation, for a sacrifice – like an animal in Abel's case – it's not because He needs it. God doesn't need food. He asks us because *we need it*. We, as His creation, need to remember WHO our blessings come from. We need to show the Creator that we love Him more than His creation. By sacrificing things back to Him, we not only show our reliance on God, but we also show Him that we are more in love with the One who gives us the blessings than we are with the blessings themselves.

Consider Christmas morning in your home. If you loved the gifts you opened more than your parents who gave them to you, you'd be like Cain. If you would rather go without gifts than without your parents, you're more like Abel.

The truth is that we make this choice all of the time: the choice between what we want, and God and what God wants for us. When we pray, it should come from our heart because we want to grow closer to God, not because we want to "get stuff" from Him. Sure, we are *supposed* to go to Mass every Sunday. After all, it's a sin to miss. But we should also go because we have a desire to be there, to worship God and to praise Him, to hear His words and receive His body and blood.

It's important to note, too, that Abel didn't give his best to God because he wanted to show up his brother. Abel didn't offer his sacrifice to gain the admiration of others or to have a great reputation. Abel gave God his best because he loved God. The same should be true for you and me. We shouldn't sing because we want our voices to sound the best. We should sing because we are truly praising God. We shouldn't go to church because we want others to think we are holy. We should go because we want to grow closer to Christ. In the end it really doesn't matter what anyone thinks of us, only what God thinks. Abel's sacrifice looked good to the world, yes; but even more meaningful to God was the motivation in Abel's heart. What's on the inside matters far more to God than what is on the outside (1 Samuel 16:7).

There is nothing you can do to make God love you more. And there is nothing you can do to make God love you less. He loves you perfectly. Going to church doesn't make God love you more. Rather, going to church helps us to love God and our brothers and sisters in Christ more. Praising God doesn't make God love you more. Rather, praising God helps us to focus less on ourselves and more on God. Serving the poor, giving money (tithing) to the Church, resisting temptation and sin, fasting or making other sacrifices doesn't make God love you more. But it does please Him since all of those things help us to grow in love and become more like Christ.

I've met plenty of people in my lifetime who loved God too little. I've never met anyone who loved God too much. Even if you are younger, you can always lead others by your holy example. Don't let being a "younger" brother or sister get in the way of leading your family closer to Christ. Don't let being an "older" sibling get in the way, either. You can always love better. You are able to be more like Abel.

ISAAC
THE BIBLE'S FIRST BARBECUE

GOD HAS A SENSE of humor. It's a fact.

Scripture says, "He who sits in the heavens, laughs" (Psalm 2:4). How can you look at an ostrich or a platypus and not, at least, smile? It takes a creative God, with a great sense of humor, to come up with a giraffe. The fact that we laugh is proof that God laughs, since we are made in His image and likeness (Genesis 1:26-27).

Now, that doesn't mean that there isn't also a time to be serious. Usually, the reason we think God lacks a sense of humor is because we're told to be quiet and respectful in His house. Obviously, we shouldn't be fooling around or be irreverent in church. At the same time, God rejoices when our laughter is holy and reverent. The point is that there is an appropriate time for everything. "There's a time to laugh" just like there is "a time to weep" (Ecclesiastes 3:4).

I was about ten years old when I learned this lesson, and I learned it the hard way. My father was working with his tools in the garage. He was swinging a hammer when he missed the nail and struck his thumb. He dropped it and started jumping up and down as he grabbed his hand in pain. Not thinking he was too hurt, I sarcastically exclaimed, "You're supposed to hit *the nail*, Dad." If you're ever in this situation, let me assure you that *this is not* a time to laugh. Making matters worse, my father angrily replied, "Do I look stupid to you?" Little did I know this would also be the day I learned the meaning of "rhetorical question." My laughter quickly turned into weeping.

There are other times in life, though, that God has a way of turning our weeping into laughter. After my grandfather's funeral, for instance, we gathered at the house and told our favorite stories of my grandpa. We sat and laughed for hours remembering joyful times and funny things he'd done. Tears are one of God's most amazing creations. Tears can show up with laughter and with pain and some-times, like at childbirth, the laughter and the pain collide.

One mother in the Bible who knew both the pain and joy of child-birth, and child raising, was Sarah. Now, Sarah and her husband, Abraham, were no ordinary couple. They were special. They were chosen to do some amazing things for God. Just because they were chosen by God, however, didn't mean that everything was easy or perfect in their lives. Sarah was not able to have children...that is, until God said it was time.

Sarah was ninety years old when she had her son, Isaac. Yes, you read that correctly. It's not a typo. She was 90, as in "she wears a lot of perfume and watches game shows," 90. In fact, when God told Abraham that Sarah was going to bear a son, Sarah (who was eavesdropping on the conversation) laughed. That's right, she *laughed at God.* As a reminder of God's incredible sense of humor, and His faithfulness, they named their son Isaac, which means laughter (Genesis 21:6).

Isaac comes from the Hebrew word *Itzah*, which means laughter

Sarah's weeping and mourning over being childless was, in an instant, turned into laughter and joy. We can learn a lot from Sarah's response. We must remember, always, that God is faithful. God works in *His time.*

Isaac's story, though, is far from over. Isaac's life is filled with both laughter and pain, with success and heroism, and with disappoint-ment and treachery. There is one story about Isaac, in particular, that has always had the ability to make me laugh and cry. It's called, "The Sacrifice of Isaac." Perhaps you've read the story before. Whether or not you are familiar with it, take a minute and read it for yourself: **Genesis 22:1-13**.

ABRAHAM AND ISAAC: THE COOK AND THE MAIN COURSE

Now, this story might leave you a little confused. You might be asking yourself, "What kind of a father would do such a thing?" or "What kind of a God would want a father to do such a thing?" Without getting too far off track, it's important to understand one thing about ancient history. Things then were not as they are now.

In those days, roughly about 2000 B.C., human sacrifice was fairly common. Some cultures believed that sacrificing their children to their (false) gods would ensure great blessings for them. So even though Abraham was following the one true God, our God, the request to sacrifice his son, Isaac, might not have seemed too crazy to Abraham, who'd seen this sort of thing before. What probably would have left Abraham confused, however, was why God would want Isaac sacrificed after all those years of childlessness, and after having Sarah conceive and give birth at such an old age.

Now that you've read the story, you might (like most people) be amazed at Abraham's faith or shocked and grateful for God's daring rescue through the angel. But what about Isaac, the main course for the Bible's first family barbecue? People don't often stop to think about what was running through poor Isaac's head that day.

Many scholars believe that Isaac was at least twelve years old when he went on this journey to Moriah with his father. In Mediterranean culture, when a boy turned twelve he was considered a young man.

Jesus was twelve years old when he went missing for three days.

If Isaac was a preteen boy, fast and full of energy, couldn't he have escaped from his elderly father that day? As Isaac watched his father set up the altar with the wood for the fire put upon it, he might have grown suspicious. Then, as he watched his father sharpen a knife with no lamb in sight, Isaac may have grown uneasy.

As he followed his father's instructions, lying down upon the altar and feeling the ropes pull tightly against his cloak; his heart must

9

have raced before eventually breaking. He may have wondered, "How could my father do this to me?" He may have thought, "Why would God, the God who my father loved and trusted, allow this?" Still, Isaac did not run. Isaac did not move. Isaac lay there in obedience. Isaac trusted Abraham who trusted God. Perfect trust brings perfect peace.

This story is not just a celebration of Abraham's obedience and trust in God. This story is, likewise, a celebration of a son's trust in his father.

Moriah means "God is my teacher" in Hebrew.

The sacrifice of Isaac is a true story. It's also a symbolic story, meaning it not only happened one day in history, but also pointed to something that was to come about two thousand years later.

You may have noticed a similarity between this story and the crucifixion of Jesus. The details of this sacrifice, the sacrifice of the father's only son, are important to note. The son, Isaac, carried the wood for the sacrifice (Genesis 22:6). The father says a lamb will be provided for sacrifice (Genesis 22:8). Years later, John the Baptist publicly declares Jesus to be the "Lamb of God" (John 1:29). The ram that is eventually sacrificed is surrounded by a thicket, a bunch of thorny branches, just like the crown Jesus wore on Good Friday (John 19:2).

What you might not know is that the "land of Moriah" (Genesis 22:2) is a small mountain range around Jerusalem that was the sight of Christ's sacrifice on the cross. Moriah is basically the same location as Calvary. The same ground that was soaked with Abraham and Isaac's tears of joy and pain would also be soaked with the blood and sweat of our Savior, Jesus, and the tears of our Mother Mary, years later.

FINDING YOUR STORY IN ISAAC'S STORY

Do you struggle with being obedient to your parents?

Do you love God above all else, even more than your family and friends?

Do you ever think that God wants you to be unhappy or to suffer?

There is no "Instruction Manual" to being a perfect parent except the Holy Bible. Countless books have been written about parenting, but the truth is that the only way to get close to being a perfect parent is by getting to know the *only perfect Parent*, God Himself.

It is difficult to be obedient to our earthly parents because we see their imperfections. Still, we are called to be obedient to them. Why? Well, because God says so, for starters (Exodus 20:12, Ephesians 6:2). Additionally, when we learn how to be obedient to our parents on earth, who we can see, it helps us learn to be more obedient to our Father in heaven, who we can't see.

For that reason, you ought to pray for two things:

First, you ought to pray, daily, for your parents. Pray that they would know God. Pray that they would serve God. Most importantly, pray that they would love God, first, with all of their heart. The more they love God, the better they will love you, too.

Second, you ought to pray to be childlike in your faith. Children who trust their parents don't consider a parent's warning or guidance to be stifling. They consider it to be freeing. For example, if my youngest daughter really trusts me when I say, "don't touch the stove," she won't think I'm trying to take away her freedom, she'll trust that I'm protecting her. If you are childlike in your faith, the Commandments won't be seen as taking away your freedom, but *freeing to you* and ensuring your holiness and happiness for years to come.

Your love for your parents should never be conditional. It should not fluctuate based on whether or not they let you do whatever you want to do. God entrusted you to your parents for this period of your life. Do everything you can to be like Isaac; trust your parents even when it doesn't seem to make sense. Continue praying to God that He will not only watch over you, but also guide them in the process.

On Mount Moriah we see two sons, Isaac and Abraham, demonstrate obedience. At that same location, Calvary, over 2,000 years later, we see the perfect obedience of another Son, Jesus. Make your home another Moriah, where your obedience and sacrifice are so visible that it becomes truly holy ground.

JOSEPH
THE BIBLE'S FIRST DAYDREAMER

HAVE YOU EVER woken up from a dream that seemed so realistic that you actually asked yourself, "Did I just dream that or did it really happen?" I once had a dream in high school in which I asked a girl from class on a date and she accepted. I remembered every part of the conversation. I remembered what time I was going to pick her up and where we planned on going. I remembered what she was wearing and what I said that made her laugh. However, the problem came two days later when I asked her for her home address and she replied, "Why do you need my home address?" I quickly made up an excuse and escaped in embarrassment.

I learned a valuable lesson that day. When a dream seems too good to be true, a good rule to avoid embarrassment is to quickly ask, "Was I dreaming?" Of course, **sometimes dreams do come true**. Years later, that girl became my wife.

Numbers 12:6 says, "If there is a prophet among you, I the LORD make myself known to him in a vision, I speak with him in a dream."

You might have big dreams for your life. They might involve money or fame or power. You might have simpler dreams for your life that include a dream job or a dream house. You might have Godly dreams for your life, like raising a holy family or serving the Church as a priest, nun, or missionary.

The Bible is filled with dreams. God often used dreams to communicate important news to people at vital times of their lives. God spoke to King Solomon, the wise men, and Jesus' earthly father, St. Joseph (just to name a few), through dreams. But long before any of these important men existed, there was another Joseph who was quite the dreamer, and dream interpreter. This Joseph you can read about in the Book of Genesis. He was the eleventh son of Jacob. And even though parents aren't supposed to play favorites, Jacob did. Joseph was his favorite son.

> **Joseph means "the Lord added."**

WHEN A DAYDREAM BECOMES A NIGHTMARE

Joseph's older brothers were, technically, his half-brothers. They all shared a father, Jacob, but the first ten boys came from three different mothers. Joseph was the firstborn son of Rachel, who was Jacob's true love. Jacob even made Joseph a special coat, "a long robe with sleeves" (Genesis 37:3). In Scripture, robes are symbolic of importance, wealth, power, and even royalty. This special gift from Joseph's father made his brothers envy and hate him.

When Joseph was about seventeen years old, his role as the favorite son became too much for his brothers to handle (Genesis 37:2). He had been telling his brothers about a series of dreams he'd been having. In one dream, for instance, the sun and the moon and eleven stars were bowing down to him. It didn't take long for his family to "interpret" what Joseph was apparently saying. "You expect us to worship you and bow down to you?" they asked through clenched teeth and curled lips.

> **Judas Iscariot betrayed Jesus for 30 pieces of silver.**

So one day when Joseph joined his brothers in the fields to shepherd the flocks, and their parents were nowhere in sight, his brothers hatched a plan to kill young Joseph. Luckily for him, one of the brothers pleaded for his life. So rather than killing Joseph, they threw him into a deep hole instead. A little later, when they saw foreign traders passing by on their way to Egypt, they decided to make a profit off of their brother and sold Joseph into slavery for 20 pieces of silver. It makes those little arguments with your siblings seem like nothing, huh?

Take a few minutes now to re-read this story right out of your Bible and see what other details jump out at you: **Genesis 37:3-34.**

Now, even though Joseph was taken to a foreign land, God was still with him and watched over him. Joseph ended up working for a high-ranking officer in the Pharaoh's courts, named Potiphar. Potiphar was impressed with Joseph and over time entrusted him with a lot of responsibility. The problem was that Joseph was a very charming and good-looking guy, and Potiphar's wife also had her eyes on him (Genesis 39:6). She made advances toward Joseph and tried to seduce him, but Joseph was a Godly man, filled with integrity and self-control (Genesis 39:7-11). He never gave in to her temptations. At one point, he even ran out of her room as she grabbed for his robe. Later, Potiphar, upon hearing about the exchange between Joseph and his wife, didn't believe Joseph's side of the story. He threw Joseph into jail. Soon after he began his jail sentence, Joseph began interpreting the dreams of his fellow prisoners and, in time, his gift for interpretation paid off.

> St. Joseph went to Egypt after a dream too (taking Mary and Jesus along with him).

When the Pharaoh began having nightmares that no one could explain, one of his officers, Joseph's old "cell mate," knew just where to look for help. All of a sudden, Joseph was standing before the Pharaoh being asked to interpret the dreams of the most powerful ruler on earth. Joseph warned that the dreams revealed a famine coming to Egypt. His interpretation set a plan in motion to prepare for the famine by storing food for several years prior. The Pharaoh was so grateful that he promoted Joseph to the highest rank in the courts. And, this all happened by the time Joseph was 30 years old (Genesis 41:46). Joseph's faithfulness to his God and to his own dignity (like the situation with Potiphar's wife) was rewarded in ways he never imagined.

> Sts. Peter and Paul also spent time in prison for loving God (see the Acts of the Apostles, chapters 5, 12 and 16).

REVENGE OR RECONCILIATION?

The story gets even better for Joseph (and his family) in the years that follow. Remember that famine that was coming to Egypt right? Well, it hit Joseph's hometown too. A few years later, Joseph's brothers journeyed south to Egypt, looking for help and for food. At one point, his older brothers who had wanted to kill him and who later sold him, ended up standing right in front of Joseph, the second most powerful man in Egypt. They didn't recognize their little daydreamer brother, though. They hadn't seen him in about 20 years and Joseph would have been cleanly shaven with shorter hair, as was the custom in Egyptian culture. Joseph, however, did recognize the hungry and filthy bunch in front of him, and was faced with a choice. Joseph had the power to send them away hungry and to get revenge for all that they had done to him. Joseph also had the power to forgive those who had wronged him. Given the kind of young man Joseph has already shown himself to be, you can probably guess which one he chose.

You can read Joseph's story with your own eyes, and you should. That's the point of the Bible, for *you to read it,* not just for others to proclaim it to you.

Take some time and read about this powerful reunion between Joseph and his brothers in **Genesis 45:1-15** and with his father Jacob (Israel) in **Genesis 46:28-47:2**.

FINDING YOUR STORY IN JOSEPH'S STORY

Have you ever felt betrayed or abandoned by the people you love the most, even your own family?

Have you ever been tempted to do wrong when "no one else was watching"?

Have you ever wanted to get revenge on someone who has wronged you?

Joseph's story might seem too "Hollywood" to relate to at first. It's a true story, a real story, better than anything you'll see on reality television. When you look a little deeper, though, past all of the drama of the murder plot, the sale into slavery, the seductive advances and jail term, the dream interpretation and famine, what you're left with is a story of heroic virtue.

Joseph loved God. Joseph loved his family. Joseph used his gifts to serve others. Joseph had respect for himself and his sexuality. Joseph had respect for women and for their sexuality. Joseph knew God hadn't abandoned him even when everyone else had.

Doing what is right is never easy, but doing what's right is always right. The sufferings that come from sin are painful, long-lasting and deadly. The suffering that comes from doing right can be painful, but it brings joy and peace and freedom. Like Joseph, when you're feeling abandoned or alone, remember that the Lord made you and that He wants good things for you. He wants to bless you, and He will if you are willing to follow His plan for your life instead of your own.

Joseph wasn't trying to brag when he shared his dreams with his family. The Lord had given Joseph a gift and he was just sharing that gift with the world. Don't play small with the world. If God has given you a gift, whether it's in music or sports, in writing or speaking, in academics or relationships, use that gift for God's glory and be humble about it.

Joseph's story reminds us, too, that even when things go wrong, God has a way of making them turn out very right if we're patient. Be patient with God. Be patient with your family. Be patient with yourself. While you might not see clearly how the story of your life will end, trust that God's plans for you are far better than anything you could dream up on your own.

MIRIAM
THE BIBLE'S FIRST BABYSITTER

WHENEVER a new babysitter comes to our home for the first time, my wife puts them through about a twenty-minute training session. It's like an army boot camp in the suburbs. She spends time explaining where diapers are kept and where bath supplies are found. She walks the sitter through the kitchen, opening the pantry and refrigerator and explaining who can eat what without getting sick. She takes the sitter through the various rooms pointing out potential safety hazards and laying down the house rules, just in case our children attempt to take advantage of the new sitter while we're out. I sit quietly until it is time for my area of expertise to be unleashed (that's when I explain how the television and all of the remotes work).

As much as I love my children, it's always more difficult for my wife to leave the kids. A mother is always concerned about "what might happen" to her child(ren) when they're out of her eyesight. Twenty minutes down the road, the mother is still worried that a child will choke on a toy or try parachuting off of the roof when the sitter isn't watching. The truth, though, is that a responsible babysitter can handle it. A good babysitter knows not to let a child out of their sight. A good babysitter is more worried about the innocent toddler than the incoming text message.

It's easy for babysitters to pay attention when they're paid to do it. When a teenager is babysitting their own sibling, however, and for no money, they don't always pay as close attention. Some older siblings think to themselves, "We're at home. He knows the rules. What could happen?" I mean, how dangerous could your own home in the suburbs be, right? How closely do you really have to watch a little brother in the safety of your own neighborhood?

What if your neighborhood, your entire country even, wasn't safe?

To read about Moses' encounter with the burning bush, read Exodus 3.

Imagine that your mom just gave birth to your new baby brother. It was a great blessing that came during a really hard time for your family. Money was tight. You lived in a home that was quite poor. Your family was living in a foreign country and the local government, who despised you because of your ethnicity, barely allowed for your family to eat. It was a violent country and time period. You had seen many of your relatives, your close family members, die from starvation, beatings, and various diseases. To make matters worse, the head of the government just issued a new law, saying that all newborn sons of your race should be taken from their parents and drowned in a river.

To read more about the Red Sea, read Exodus 18.

This situation might sound insane and unrealistic, but it happened. In fact, this was the setting that Moses was born into. You've heard of Moses. You might remember how God spoke to Moses through a burning bush. You probably recall the story of Moses leading God's people, the Israelites, through the Red Sea. You remember how God gave Moses the two tablets containing the Ten Commandments.

To read more about the Ten Commandments, read Exodus 20.

Long before any of these events, though, Moses was in great danger. The Pharaoh decreed that all sons born to Hebrew women should be taken and thrown into the Nile. Moses' mother acted courageously and swiftly, though. She gave birth to Moses and hid him from the Egyptians for three full months. When she could no longer hide him, she placed him in a basket woven out of branches and floated him down the Nile River. Like any good mother, though, she couldn't just abandon him, so she asked Moses' older sister, Miriam, to keep an eye on the basket, making her the Bible's first official babysitter (Exodus 2:4).

She walked along the banks of the Nile, following the basket holding her baby brother. Eventually Moses' basket found its way to shore just as the Pharaoh's daughter was taking a bath in the waters. The Pharaoh's daughter saw the baby and, realizing it was a Hebrew child, decided to secretly save his life and raise him as her own son. She brought the baby out of the Nile and found a Hebrew mother to nurse him. The coolest part of the story is that the woman selected to care for Moses until he was older turned out to be his actual mother!

The name "Moses" means "to draw out of the water."

At this point of the story, Miriam disappears for a while. When we see her again, years later, Moses had already been called by God to be a prophet. Moses was told to lead the Israelites out of Egypt and his brother, Aaron, and sister, Miriam, were right by his side to lead.

SOME BABYSITTERS MAKE A "PROPHET"(ESS)

Prophets hold a very important place in the Bible. In fact, a large chunk of the Bible consists of the writings of the prophets. The prophets were not magicians or fortune-tellers. They were ordinary people called to share extraordinary things.

The word "Prophet" means "mouthpiece."

Miriam was the first "prophetess" listed in Scripture. While we aren't exactly sure what God told her to say, the Book of Exodus lists her with this title and great honor (Ex. 15:20). It seems, though, that after some time, Miriam might have gotten a "big head" over her role.

Sometime after Moses received the Ten Commandments, while the Israelites were wandering through the desert, Miriam disagreed with the way her younger brother Moses was leading and disliked the way things were going.

Take a few minutes and slowly read the scene for yourself: **Numbers 12:1-16**.

Miriam had become very self-focused. "Hasn't the Lord also spoken through us?" she asked. Basically, the older sister was looking at her younger brother and wondering, "What makes him so special?" Miriam's jealousy, though, didn't kill Moses as Cain's did Abel. Nor did it enslave her little brother as Joseph's brothers had done to him. No, Miriam's jealousy only enslaved herself.

God's punishment of leprosy was not as painful as what it brought with it. Leprosy meant you were no longer part of the community. At the time, Lepers had to remove themselves from the rest of the community, so as not to contaminate anyone else with their disease. This punishment was far worse than Miriam's skin becoming white and flaky and contagious. This punishment left Miriam, once a respected leader, all alone and without the love of her friends and family.

Miriam was entrusted with much, but she abused the power and trust that both God and the people had placed in her. The minute she started thinking about what she deserved, rather than what God deserved, the people following began to suffer. The physical effects of leprosy were plain to see as Miriam walked on the outskirts of camp for that week. The truest effects of gossip and mistrust, however, are always far deeper. Even Miriam's whitened skin could not compare to how much pain she was feeling in her heart, after hearing God compare her action to a "spit in the face" (Exodus 12:14).

God punished her for her own good. God taught Miriam a lesson as good parents are often forced to do. The leprosy helped Miriam to appreciate the importance of community. It taught her humility and it helped her grow in love, not spite, for her God who had already given her so much.

FINDING YOUR STORY IN MIRIAM'S STORY

Do you ever feel like you don't get the attention that you deserve?

Do you struggle with wanting others to notice you or listen to you?

Do you ever gossip about others with the desire for them, or you, to be seen differently?

We can learn a lot from Miriam. Miriam was entrusted with a great deal of responsibility. We can learn how important it is to watch out for both our little brothers and sisters in our families and our little brothers and sisters in the faith. We need to protect them. We need to offer a good example to them.

We can also learn that words have power. If the words we use are designed to build God's Kingdom, He blesses them and lives are saved. If the words we use tear down the Kingdom by tearing down others, He does not bless them and, eventually, we'll be without community.

Usually when we talk about gossip, we hear about how painful the effects can be on the victim. Gossip has the power to destroy a person. But what about the person or people who are gossiping? Why do so many people do it?

Some people are nosey. Some people are bored. Some people are judgmental, and others are just rude. Most of the time, though, the one thing that gossipers have in common is that deep down, they don't like themselves. Rather than focus their energy on improving themselves, they tear down other people. It makes them feel superior when they find faults in others without having to focus on their own.

Gossip is one of the greatest tools of the devil, in his attempts to destroy Christ's Kingdom on earth.

To read more about the dangers of gossip, try James 3:5-10, 14.

All that being said, it's normal to want to be heard. It's human to desire respect. It's not wrong to want others to see that you are special or that you have something to say. The question is whether you want attention for your own glory or for God's. God can and will use you, even as a prophet, to live and speak in His name, but not for your glory or fame. God wants others to know Him and His perfect love. If you want to be heard and noticed and remembered, live for God, which will have people talking about you a whole lot longer. People will remember you for how much you loved Him.

As you take a more active role in your faith, you're going to find yourself in some tough situations from time to time. Sometimes it is better not to say anything at all and just to preach by a holy example. Don't forget the fact that "actions do speak louder than words." On the other hand, a lot of times, if you don't speak up in certain situations because you're uncomfortable, then God's truth will go unspoken.

DAVID
THE BIBLE'S FIRST ROCK STAR

THE LEAD SINGER for U2, Bono, once compared King David to Elvis Presley. He said that David was as close to a rock star as a Bible character could get. The more I think about it, Bono had a pretty good point.

David was a talented musician who not only played music, but who also wrote it. He came from a pretty small town called Bethlehem, which might sound familiar. And his "career" began with him being an innocent, beloved young hero to millions; but along the way, some bad decisions caused him a lot of pain and broken relationships.

Before we get ahead of ourselves, though, let's take a second and see how much you remember about this Biblical "rock star."

David is one of the most famous leaders in the history of mankind. He is one of the most important figures in the entire Bible. David was also one of the most powerful men to ever walk the earth. Oh, and David was a sinner.

You may know the story of David. You might know that he is an ancestor of Jesus. You might have heard about how he was a shepherd or the youngest son of a man named Jesse. You might even know that the prophet Samuel anointed David with oil when he was still a very young man, probably a teenager, and that the Spirit of the Lord "came mightily upon David" (1 Sam. 16:13).

> **David's anointing with oil and reception of the Spirit is a lot like what happens to you at Confirmation.**

You've almost definitely heard about his fight with Goliath, the mightiest warrior of the Philistine army. David wasn't looking for a fight; he was a shepherd boy. He was just dropping off some lunch to his older brothers, who were in Israel's army. They were the warriors, not David.

Take a minute and read the story on your own: **1 Samuel 17:1-54**.

David means "beloved."

Things changed for David that day, as you can see. It only took one rock from the teen's slingshot and the fight was over. This was no *Ultimate Fighting Challenge.* This was no challenge at all. Goliath was cocky, thinking that his strength could outmatch God's. Goliath had a big head...until David cut it off. God's blessing was upon David; and when God's favor is upon you, there's nothing you cannot do (Luke 1:37, Philippians 4:13).

While that victory was amazing and it began David's long and impressive career as a warrior, he did far more than just fight. David is also credited with writing most of the Psalms in the Bible.

BEHIND THE MUSIC

Psalm 23 sounds like something a shepherd would write. Read it for yourself.

Songs tell a lot about the songwriter. When you listen to a song you can tell what the songwriter is thinking or feeling, or what they want you to think they are feeling. There are 150 psalms in the Bible, mostly attributed to King David. They say a lot about the author, David, but even more about the Author of Life, God.

Psalms are songs that praise or call out to God. We hear or sing a psalm in almost every single Catholic Mass; the psalm follows the first reading. You'll notice that the words and cries of some psalms sound very joyful while others sound absolutely miserable. David wrote about the highs and lows of life because David's life was a series of highs and lows. Just to offer you a few examples:

- His best friend's dad wanted him dead.
- His first wife was embarrassed and ashamed of him.
- He was the mightiest ruler and warrior on earth.
- His army was powerful and his kingdom was far-reaching but they were constantly under attack.
- He betrayed his loyal servant and had him killed.
- His own son wanted him dead.

> You can read about David's life in 1 & 2 Samuel, 1 Kings and 1 Chronicles.

These might not be situations you can relate to at your age. These are hopefully not situations you'll ever have to relate to in your own life, *at any age*. There is one afternoon in David's life, in particular, that you might be able to relate to very well.

GOD STILL SEES WHEN "NO ONE ELSE IS LOOKING"

The Bible says it was "late one afternoon" when David got off his couch (1 Samuel 11:2). He was alone. His armies were off fighting, but he had remained back at the King's palace. When he walked onto his rooftop, he looked around and was quickly shocked as he saw something (someone): a woman bathing in a pool of water.

It was at this moment that David had a choice.

He could look away to protect her dignity and his own chastity, or he could let his eyes go where they didn't need to go. He could choose holiness or sin. He was standing at the crossroads of temptation. Rather than looking away and choosing the honorable and manly thing to do, David was selfish. He stared at the bathing woman. He allowed his own lust to get the better of him. David allowed the lust to overtake him. He then used his power to send for the woman. Her name was Bathsheba. She was the wife of Uriah, an armor-bearer in King David's army. After he summoned her to his palace, King David sinned even further, having sex with Bathsheba before sending her home. Later, when he learned that Uriah was her husband, David sinned, yet again, hatching a plan for Uriah to be killed in battle so that Bathsheba could be his and his alone.

How did this all happen? How did David go from being the "anointed one", the one with whom God was so pleased, to the one who was so selfish, so lustful, and even murderous?

FINDING YOUR STORY IN DAVID'S STORY

Have you ever done something you knew you weren't supposed to do?

Have you ever looked at something you knew you shouldn't look at or watch?

Have you ever done something you're ashamed of in an effort to "cover up" something else you'd done?

The internet is an amazing invention. You can find information on almost anything within seconds. Research for a class paper that used to take your parents or grandparents hours or even weeks to find in a library, is now available to you within a click or two. There is no shortage of things for you to read, to listen to, or to watch online, but that doesn't mean that everything online will bring you closer to God.

You know as well as anyone, probably even better than your parents or grandparents, how many "dark" things online will actually lead you into shame and sin instead of leading you to light, joy and freedom.

Pornography destroys people. Pornography destroys men *and* women. It degrades women. It degrades men, too. Pornography begins with lust. It begins with taking advantage of other people. It begins with the desire to look where you shouldn't look. Long before the internet or cable television, lust was still a struggle. In fact, one of the most famous stories of sin in the entire Bible happened when a powerful man, King David, was looking where he shouldn't have been.

Maybe you can relate. Maybe you know the temptation of looking where you shouldn't, at things that you shouldn't. Maybe you know, too, the guilt and shame that comes from looking at pornography or taking in other media that destroys your soul. That's what sin does: it replaces freedom with slavery, life with death.

You're not alone.

We all sin. We all fall short of God's hopes and expectations for us. We may be tempted at different times and in different ways, but we are all tempted to sin in some way. We have that in common. You're not the only one who is tempted. You're not the only one who sins. Your parents were tempted. Your grandparents were tempted. The Pope is tempted. Your parish priest is tempted. Your teachers and your coaches are tempted, too. Adam and Eve were tempted (and you know how that turned out). Even Jesus was tempted, but Jesus didn't sin.

God knew you'd be tempted. He also knows that you can resist all temptations with His help. Check out what it says in **1 Corinthians 10:13**:

> *"No temptation has overtaken you that is not common to man. God is faithful, and he will not let you be tempted beyond your strength, but with the temptation will also provide the way of escape, that you may be able to endure it."*

Did you notice what God said there? He didn't say you wouldn't be tempted, He said you won't be overcome by it. He says that no temptation is beyond your strength because God always provides a way out if you call on Him. He is promising you that you can withstand and endure even the hardest temptations. Not because of how strong *you are*, but because of how strong **He is**.

> To "repent" means to turn away from sin (darkness) and turn back to God (light).

Yes, David sinned. David also repented. He was sincerely sorry for what he had done and he went to the Lord to make it right. If you've sinned, trust in God's mercy. There is no sin

David's prayer of repentance can be found in Psalm 51. You might recognize it from Mass.

too big for God to forgive. The only sin God won't forgive is the sin you don't ask forgiveness for. God doesn't force His mercy on anyone, but He's dying to give you His mercy. That's what the crucifix is: living proof that God is dying for you to know how much He loves you.

Take advantage of the Sacrament of Reconciliation. Be honest with yourself. Be honest with the priest. There you can sit with Jesus Christ, in the person of your parish priest, and ask Him for the help you need to defeat temptation and conquer your sins. If you struggle with pornography, admit it. Allow the grace of the Sacrament to give you strength to start over clean and pure.

Only Christ is perfect. Jesus is the one we look to for our example. We seek to be like Jesus, not just to be like athletes or celebrities or even rock stars. Jesus is the one who we need to pattern our lives after.

JOSIAH
THE BIBLE'S FIRST PRETEEN KING

AS I LAY there coughing and hacking in my bed,
I had no one to blame but myself. My throat was so sore I couldn't
even swallow water. My head felt like a hot-air balloon and I couldn't
breathe through my nose. I caught the worst cold I'd ever had and
it was all my fault. I got sick because I cared more about what my
friends thought than what my mother said.

I was in seventh grade at the time, meeting a bunch of friends at
the mall to see a movie. Afraid that they would see me get out of my
mother's minivan, I asked her to drop me off about a mile down the
street from the entrance. The forecast called for rain, but I didn't
care. There could have been a volcano erupting in the mall parking
lot, for all I cared. Not only was I idiotic, I was stubborn. My mother
pleaded with me to let her pull up closer, but I said no way. We got
into a huge argument over it. I said some hurtful things and let my
mother know how embarrassed I was of her. To this day, I regret how
I treated her that afternoon. My behavior was the embarrassment,
not her.

I was in a t-shirt and shorts that day as the cold front and the even-
tual thunderstorm came through. I walked through the rain, getting
doused by cars driving through the puddles on the street. I arrived at
the movies so soaked that I was shaking. My reputation was intact,
but my respiratory system was destroyed. The air conditioning was
on in the theater, making matters even worse. And, during moments
of silence in the movie, if you listened closely enough, you could
actually hear the water dripping off of my shorts onto the popcorn-
covered floor below.

It was the longest movie of my life. The closing credits could not
get there fast enough. That night I felt the sickness creep in and, as
expected, I was miserably sick for the next several days. Even more

miserable than the sickness in my body, though, was the sickness I was feeling in my soul. I wasn't really ashamed of my mom, far from it. I loved my mom. I just wasn't mature enough to admit it or show it. In my effort to "be a man," I acted like a bratty little boy.

Middle school brings natural struggles along with it. Your body is constantly changing. Hormones roll around inside of you like a pinball machine plugged into a nuclear accelerator. Girls develop at a rapid rate. Boys begin a semester four feet tall and end it 6'5". Voices change. Complexions change. Friendships change. Relationships change. Family dynamics often change, too.

Some of the middle school youths I meet have great relationships with their parents. They eat together, hang out together and they consider their parents their heroes. Other middle school youths I meet act just like I did: they're embarrassed, annoyed, angry, outspoken, and disrespectful. In short, they seldom stop to think about how their words or actions affect their family. They focus on the "I" in f-a-m-i-l-y.

If they only knew, like I do now, how blessed they are to even have a family, they might act differently. Now, as a parent, I understand two things: first, I'll never be a perfect parent but I can be a holy parent; second, my kids will never truly know how much I love them and I can never tell them enough.

Most of the time when a teen or pre-teen is ashamed of, or embarrassed by, their family, it's without a good reason. Just because a parent acts dorky or might not dress very hip is no reason to be embarrassed by them. If you want to talk about a kid who had a reason to be embarrassed by his family tree, look no further than the Bible's first preteen king: Josiah.

Josiah means "the Lord supports."

NOT YOUR AVERAGE JO(SIAH)

Josiah became King of Judah when he was only eight years old. Can you imagine that? Imagine being made President of the United States at eight years old. The only catch is that you weren't elected, you were given the throne even though your family name was tarnished and you were already considered a horrible person because of your ancestors. Not the best way to start your term as a leader of a nation, huh?

You see, Josiah's family tree gives all new meaning to the term "dysfunctional family." Josiah's grandpa, King Manasseh, didn't just believe in false gods, he celebrated them. Manasseh built altars to false gods and worshipped them inside the Lord's temple. Manasseh sacrificed one of his own sons in a fire, practiced witchcraft and other forms of evil arts, murdered innocent people, and led an entire kingdom of followers away from the one, true God (2 Kings 21:9).

How's that for a messed up family tree? Wait, it gets worse.

Following Grandpa Manasseh, Josiah's father, King Amon, continued in the same horrible footsteps. King Amon also worshipped false gods, just like his dad. He, too, abandoned the Lord and was so evil that eventually his own followers killed him in his own house. It was at that time that young Josiah was named King, carrying with him all kinds of family baggage. Something really interesting happened, though, when Josiah was only a teenager.

Read it for yourself: **2 Chronicles 34:1-7**.

Now, did you notice how old Josiah was when he began "to seek after the Lord" (verse 3)? It was in the eighth year of his reign. Josiah was only *sixteen years old* when he stood up and turned his country upside down.

> **Josiah's life is also found in 2 Kings 22-23.**

Josiah's family tree was anything but glorious. Yet, rather than letting his father's or his grandfather's sins dictate the path of his life, Josiah went further back into his family tree, until he found someone he could look up to. He found King David, whom we've already discussed. While David was not perfect, he was a man "after

> **Josiah made a public covenant to follow the Lord and His Commandments.**

> **The Prophet Jeremiah wrote a lamentation over Josiah's death (2 Chron. 35:25).**

the Lord's own heart." Josiah needed a hero, a role model, and he found one.

As a teenager, he tore down the altars to false gods, smashed statues of idols and restored the Temple for proper worship. He prayed the Scriptures, reinstituted and lived out God's law, honored the sacred feast days and renewed the covenant. He was a humble, prayerful man. Josiah was holy and bold and turned his whole heart to God. In the process, Josiah saved an entire nation from ruin.

The young king understood three things that many of us forget:

1. The pursuit of true holiness is contagious.
2. Humility is a strong weapon in the hands of God.
3. You cannot let your past or your family's past, ruin your present or dictate your future.

Josiah went on to reign for thirty-one years and when he died, an entire nation mourned his death (2 Chronicles 35:24-25). So heroic and beloved was Josiah that hundreds of years later they were still praising his name.

FINDING YOUR STORY IN JOSIAH'S STORY

How does your family tree compare to Josiah's?

Do you let your age or lack of knowledge keep you from speaking out for God or living for Him more boldly?

Have you ever allowed past failings to make you doubt your present ability or future holiness?

Regardless of how old you are or how blessed or messed up your family tree might seem, God desires a great life for you (John 10:10). You might come from a family or a past with a lot of darkness, sin or pain. If so, it's even more important that you do what Josiah did: look around for holy lives you can pattern your own after. It doesn't matter how young you are; you can live a holy, saintly life today and every day that you walk with the Lord.

You cannot control many of the circumstances in your life. You cannot control if your parents go to church, if they pray, if they teach you about the faith. You can, however, *invite them* to go to Mass with you or to pray with you or to learn about the faith with you.

If you are holding any grudges or pain, forgive your family members and friends. If you, like me, have caused any pain to others through your words or actions, seek their forgiveness. Remember, parents may not love you perfectly <u>but they do love you</u>. At the very least, you can pray for your family daily. If you are fortunate enough to come from a holy family, thank God for it and affirm your family for trying to follow God each day. Look around your parish, your youth group, your school and find people who are truly trying to live holy lives and affirm them, too. Thank them for their example.

Remember that you are never too young to lead others to God through your words and, more powerfully, through your actions. Your life is the greatest invitation others will ever receive to follow the Lord. And on those dark and stormy days, when the heavens open and the rains fall hard, your example will call others out of the rain, away from sickness (sin) and into the warmth and love that only a parent (God) can offer.

ESTHER
THE BIBLE'S FIRST BEAUTY QUEEN

GROWING UP with older brothers, you have to learn how to "take it." In my house, from the minute I could walk I was sort of a slave. My brothers were constantly telling me to go and get them things. If I refused (and if my Mom wasn't within hearing distance), I would suffer their wrath. Sometimes it was a wet willy, and sometimes it was sitting on my chest and dangling spit over my face. At other times, it was a good old-fashioned punch in the arm. As if the physical torture wasn't enough, there was also the teasing. No matter what I said they could find a way to make fun of it. They were older, smarter, and stronger than I was.

As time went on, though, I developed a pretty quick wit. I had to in order to survive. I learned how to defend myself verbally long before I could defend myself physically. I developed a thick skin, too. Kids at school didn't bother me. Nothing they said could compare to the brotherly abuse I'd received at home. Other kids weren't so lucky. I remember watching some classmates get made fun of on the bus ride to school each day. They were quiet or shy and the older kids took advantage of it. Most days I just kept quiet, thankful that I wasn't the one getting teased. After a while, though, I grew tired of watching it happen. The Lord may not have blessed my fifth grade frame with huge muscles, but He had blessed me with brothers who had taught me how to stand up to bullying.

One day, on the bus, I couldn't take it anymore. Two eighth grade boys were making fun of a girl named Danielle. Now, Danielle was a really sweet girl, the kind of girl who would never make fun of someone else. She was smart, soft-spoken, and always nice to people. Danielle was also a beautiful girl with some facial scarring and disfigurement from being horribly burned as a young child. On this day, the boys were making fun of her clothes (which was incredibly stupid since we were all in school uniforms); they were making fun of her hair; and they were making fun of her scars. Just as I was about to say something, we pulled up to the school and everyone exited the bus. I noticed Danielle trying to fight back tears, but she couldn't. They streamed down her face as she collected her books and bag. That was it.

I leapt off the bus and followed the eighth grade idiots into the school parking lot. I threw down my backpack and unleashed a verbal tirade of righteous anger on them. Kids gathered around. The bus driver quickly exited the bus and tried to calm me down. Teachers came running. Still, I didn't stop. I tore them down the same way they had torn down Danielle. I insulted their looks. I mocked their haircuts. I made fun of their grades, their lack of athletic ability and their lack of girlfriends. I mocked every level of their personality until they were both fighting back tears in front of all of their friends. They couldn't even fight back. They were left speechless.

At that moment I felt a hand grab my arm. I swung around expecting it to be a teacher or, worse yet, one of their friends. Instead, I saw Danielle standing there. "Mark, stop it," she said, "this isn't right."

"Huh?" I thought. Why wasn't she happy? I was defending *her* and every other student who'd been made fun of by these eighth grade bullies. This isn't how my "movie moment" was supposed to turn out! Shouldn't I have been lifted up on the shoulders of the other students? No, my story ended with me in the Principal's office and half of the eighth grade students waiting for me at lunchtime. While I was right in wanting to speak up and defend Danielle's honor, I went about it all wrong. I let my anger get the better of me. I didn't use my head. I didn't act like a Christian in the situation because I didn't pray. I failed to love my "enemies." Trying to protect others with no concern for yourself is heroic, indeed, but not if it violates Jesus' commandment to love. Love for God must be primary.

Esther means "star" in Persian.

The Bible is filled with heroic people who stood up to bullying, heroic people who loved and saved others through their self-sacrifice. Jesus is the primary example of heroism. A few hundred years before Jesus' birth, however, there lived another hero (a heroine, actually) who is one of the most courageous women in all of Scripture.

She was the Bible's first beauty queen, and her name was Esther.

ESTHER'S STORY

Esther was born at a difficult time in Israel's history. You see, long after all of the Kings, including King David and King Josiah, Jerusalem was destroyed and most of the Jewish people were deported as slaves to Babylon. Soon after, Babylon was taken over by Persia. The Jewish people were thousands of miles from their home, living under a foreign ruler and treated as second-class citizens.

This is hard for us in the United States to imagine. We live in a free and powerful country. Even though there is still racial and religious persecution in various parts of the country, most Americans still live freely, enjoying basic human rights in a democracy. Imagine, though, living in a culture where you had no rights to speak of and where your race and your religious background left you in danger.

Esther's Hebrew name is "Hadassah."

This was the time into which Esther was born. She was an orphan growing up in a foreign land (Persia) and was raised by her distant cousin, Mordecai. Now Esther was exceptionally beautiful, which was both a blessing and a curse (Esther 2:7).

The Persian queen publicly embarrassed her husband, King Ahasuerus, and as a result, the king began looking for a new bride. Because of Esther's great beauty, she was one of the young women quickly gathered for the king. Esther was taken to the palace for preparation and training, with the potential of becoming the next queen of Persia. It was the Bible's own version of a beauty pageant.

Ahasuerus is the Hebrew form of the name "Xerxes."

Esther caught King Ahasuerus' eye and, eventually, became his new queen. In this culture, however, she was in no way equal to the king.

The film *One Night with the King* (2006) is a re-telling of the Book of Esther.

In fact, Queen Esther could only approach the king or enter his court when summoned by him. Any other attempt to approach him was punishable by death. To make matters worse, there was an incredibly evil man named Haman, the prime minister and a high-ranking commander in the king's court, who hated the Jewish people.

One day as Haman walked by, Mordecai refused to bow to Haman, as was prescribed by law. Haman was furious and so he ordered Mordecai to be put to death. But, he didn't stop there. Much like Hitler, Haman was a madman bent on the destruction of the Jewish people. He quickly hatched a plan to kill all of the Jews by manipulating King Ahasuerus.

When Mordecai learned of the Jewish peoples' fate, he secretly contacted Queen Esther, asking her to approach the king and to save their people. Queen Esther was now faced with a dilemma:

Ashes and sackcloth were symbols of mourning and repentance. This is why we have ashes on Ash Wednesday.

If she approached King Ahasuerus without being summoned, she could be charged with contempt in the king's court, publicly embarrassing him (as had the former queen) and be sentenced to death. If she did nothing, her beloved cousin and guardian, Mordecai, would be put to to death and the Jewish people would be destroyed.

So Queen Esther prayed. She asked that all of the Jews in the city, Mordecai included, join her in prayer and in fasting for her impending visit to the king. Read for yourself the bravery and holiness of this courageous young woman: **Esther 4:1-17.**

On the third day of fasting, Queen Esther rose up from the ashes and sackcloth, prepared herself, and entered the court of King Ahasuerus. Each step she took was not only proof of her trust in God, but of her courage and selflessness. In the following chapters in the Book of

Esther, you can (and should) read of Queen Esther's brilliant plot to both save her people and ensure that Haman would not harm anyone ever again. Mordecai had raised Queen Esther to worship the one true God and not the false gods of the Persians. When it mattered most, it was Esther's intense love for her God and for her people that allowed her to save the day by doing what no one thought possible.

FINDING YOUR STORY IN ESTHER'S STORY

Have you ever been the victim of bullying?

Have you ever been afraid to speak up, fearing what might happen to you if you do?

What are some situations, even small ones, in which God is calling you to be more heroic?

We live in a world that is obsessed with outward beauty and physical power. The lesson I learned on the bus that day, however, is the same lesson that Esther learned thousands of years prior: *true* beauty and *true* power come from God's Spirit within you.

Esther's outer beauty might have turned heads, but in the end it was Esther's inner beauty, her love for God and for her people, that saved souls. Danielle's outer beauty may have been "scarred," but in the end she proved to be the most beautiful person on that bus. She taught me a lot that day about how to love all people, even your enemies.

When we are baptized and confirmed, we receive the power of the Holy Spirit. This might not seem like a big deal to some on earth, but it is a very big deal in heaven. Through the Sacraments, God's life (grace) fills you. The Holy Spirit dwells within you, and that makes you beautifully dangerous and wonderfully powerful (Philippians 4:13).

You are not all that different from Esther. You live in a culture where people are constantly being destroyed. You might be destroyed by classmates bullying you at school. You might be destroyed by the need to physically measure up to the airbrushed supermodels on magazine covers. You live in a culture where almost fifty million babies have been destroyed through legalized abortion, while millions of Christians say nothing about it.

Esther was a young woman who God put in the right place at the right time. God had her right where He wanted her. God has you right where He wants you, too. For others to be saved, Esther had to tap into the Spirit of God within her. Esther had the power. She only had to pray to unleash it. You have the power, too. Are you courageous enough to unleash it? Do you love others enough to put yourself on the line?

There are people, from the unborn to the elderly, who are in need of the love of God working through you. God gave you the Holy Spirit, "a Spirit of power and love and self-control" (2 Timothy 1:7). Unleash that power with a loving heart and you, too, will be known throughout heaven and earth for your heroism.

MARY

THE BIBLE'S FIRST (AND ONLY) PREGNANT VIRGIN

I HATED chores growing up. Vacuuming was a
pain. Doing dishes was an annoyance. Folding laundry was no fun.
Mowing the grass was miserable. Shoveling snow was even worse. I
began looking for the easiest way out of chores. I would eat less, hoping for fewer dishes. I would wear clothes out of my hamper to cut
down on laundry. I did my best to cram trash into the container as
hard as I could, hoping that by the time it was overflowing it would
be my brother's turn to take it out.

I did my chores every week, though, because I was told to do them.
I did them for my allowance. I did them to avoid punishment. But
when my mother was pregnant and sick, and she was unable to take
care of us or take care of the house, my motivation changed. I finally
did the chores entrusted to me, for the right reason; I did them out
of love. It didn't mean that the tasks I had to do became more fun or
that they didn't include discomfort. After all, yard work is never comfortable, as Adam would tell you (Genesis 3:17-19). It just meant that
I endured the discomfort with less whining and with a better attitude
because of my love for my parents. Let's be honest, no discomfort I
went through could compare to a pregnant woman's, as Eve would
tell you (Genesis 3:16).

Since the time of my mother's pregnancy, my attitude towards chores
changed for good. I had learned a lesson. As much sacrifice as it took
for me to do them, I saw what my mother had gone through to have
my little brother. She had sacrificed way more. In fact, my parents
had sacrificed many things so that their children could have many
things. Chores taught me a lot about discipline and about being part
of a family. My parents taught me a lot about self-reliance and hard
work through having me do these chores. They also taught me a lot
about self-sacrifice and true love by expecting more from me than I
was comfortable with.

God, too, believes in us more than we believe in ourselves. He knows what we are designed for. He knows all that we are capable of in this life. He knows the necessity of discipline and the importance of obedience. God is a parent who knows that true love is seen in sacrifice. Look at the cross. That is a Son who lives in loving obedience and a Father who knows about a loving sacrifice. Near the cross, too, was another parent who understood the love that sacrifice requires and the pain that can come with it.

> **The name Mary is a shorter form of the name Miriam, meaning bitterness.**

She was the one soul who was central to Jesus' plan of salvation, a soul that was set apart by God from the beginning so that she could fulfill a unique role. God preserved the Virgin Mary from sin, properly known as the Immaculate Conception. He designed Mary for a specific role, the highest privilege given anyone who has ever lived. Mary became God's perfect dwelling place on earth. This was the vocation she was uniquely suited for and her "yes" to God had eternal effects.

JUST AN ORDINARY DAY IN NAZARETH

> **The name Mary could also mean "wished for a child" or "drop of the sea."**

St. Luke begins the story of "The Annunciation" by telling us that God sent the angel Gabriel to the town of Nazareth to a virgin (Luke 1:26-27). The Bible doesn't tell us what the Blessed Virgin Mary was doing at the moment the angel appeared. Tradition tells us that Mary was a teenager, probably about 14 years old. And since it wasn't the Sabbath (a day set aside when you were not allowed to work), it makes sense that Mary was probably doing her daily chores.

Life in Galilee was not easy. Men worked hard in their respective trades of fishing, farming or carpentry (like St. Joseph). Women worked equally hard, having to draw water from the well and transport it home, tending to the children, the house and the animals, all while making meals over a small fire. Children were expected to work hard, too. The "chores" of a child from Jesus' time were more like full time jobs.

Mary was raised by holy parents and knew her Sacred Scripture. She prayed constantly. Her work was a form of prayer. Even as prayerful and as well versed as she was in the Hebrew Scriptures, she could not have been prepared for an extraordinary encounter with a super-natural visitor.

Tradition tells us that Mary's parents were Sts. Joachim and Anne.

Picture the scene: Mary is working in the house, possibly on her knees cleaning or preparing food in the kitchen, when all of the sudden there is a flash of light. She looks up to see a glorious, almost blinding, presence.

Imagine the room. Envision the angel. Close your eyes and really see our Mother Mary and the angel Gabriel. Now, slowly read **Luke 1:26-38** and pay attention to the details of the story.

Ave Maria literally means "Hail Mary!"

The Archangel's first word to Mary is "Hail!" Now, this doesn't mean "What's up?" or "How ya' doing?" No, the Greek word for "Hail!" meant "Rejoice!" The news that the angel brought was not only good news, it was great news! Mary had a reason to rejoice and so do we. God's mission to save us was kicking into high gear, and that rescue mission was going to occur through a fourteen-year old virgin from a tiny, rural town.

The angel then says a phrase that had never been uttered before, proclaiming Mary to be "full of grace" (Luke 1:28). Nowhere in the Old Testament had anyone ever been addressed like this. In fact, this is the only time in the Bible that an angel addresses someone with a title and not just his or her name. Grace can best be described as "God's life in us." Mary was so filled with God's life from the begin-ning, even before this encounter, that she was the only one worthy of such a title. Also, Gabriel's proclamation of "the Lord is with you," must have been comforting to Mary since a life-changing meeting with an angel probably wasn't on her list of chores to do that day.

As Gabriel goes on to share the great news about God's Son taking flesh in her womb, he reminds her not to fear. Throughout the Bible when the Creator draws near to His creation, He must calm our hearts and remind us not to fear Him. Mary was no different. She wasn't so much scared as she was overcome with awe and overwhelmed with a question.

"And Mary said to the angel, 'How shall this be, since I have no husband?'" (Luke 1:34)

The Blessed Virgin Mary is "Immaculate" which comes from the Latin word for "unstained" or "sinless."

Twice before we are told that Mary is a virgin (1:27). So Mary's question is more about her being a virgin than it is about her being unmarried, though she was betrothed or promised to St. Joseph. Mary didn't doubt God's ability or promise; she was trying to figure out how it was going to work.

Thanks to the overabundance of grace that God granted to Mary from the moment of her own immaculate conception, she was absolutely capable of the mission she was about to undertake.

The Rosary helps us focus on Jesus' life through the eyes and heart of Mary.

Mary's last words to the angel were the most beautiful words ever uttered by any teenager in history:

"Behold, I am the handmaid of the Lord; let it be to me according to your word." (Luke 1:38)

In that one line, Mary proclaimed it all. God comes first. We are His servants and she was His handmaid. What God wants comes first. God's plan for Mary came first. She trusted Him completely. She trusted His plan wholeheartedly. She didn't know what would come next. She wasn't sure how it was all going to work. She just knew that she was filled with God's life and that she shouldn't fear because God had a plan! So she said yes with every part of her soul and changed history forever. Mary turned in her teenage duties for a baby deity.

FINDING YOUR STORY IN MOTHER MARY'S STORY

Have you ever felt like God expected too much from you?

Are you afraid that God's calling for you might include suffering?

Do you rejoice each day that God knows you and loves you?

Do you trust God enough to let Him be in complete control of your life?

It might be difficult for you to compare your life to Mary's life. She was a pregnant virgin at fourteen. She had to tell her fiancé that God was the father of her child. She had to travel almost 100 miles in her third trimester of pregnancy and give birth in the filthiest of settings. After Jesus' birth, Mary had a prophet tell her that she was going to suffer tremendously. She had random astrologers from thousands of miles away show up with gifts, wanting to worship her baby boy. Then, Mary, Joseph, and Jesus had to escape to a foreign country when the king went on a murdering rampage, looking for her newborn son.

Mary is different. She's unique in every way. She is God's own Mother. She is a virgin, pure and sinless, and the perfect model of chastity. She is filled with God's life (grace) and is a part of God's salvation plan of for us all. Oh, and one more thing, Mary is not just Jesus' mother, she's your mother too (John 19:27).

It might seem like Mary is as far from you as you are from heaven, but that's not entirely true. Through the Sacraments, specifically the Eucharist, we are also filled with God's grace. God has a plan for you. Your life will play a role in the salvation of others. Your life will have suffering. And, your life will have incredible joy if you know Christ intimately and follow God daily, as Mary did.

The Lord is with you.

That's right, the Lord wasn't just with Mary; *He is with you!* He is with you in the Sacraments, in His Word, in the priesthood, in the Church. The Holy Spirit is God, and the Holy Spirit lives within you. So you, not unlike Mary, are filled with God's grace. And also, like Mary, God has a plan for your life. His plan will include suffering at times, but it's in those times we need to lean into the grace that God offers us and remember the words that Mary heard that incredible day, "Do not be afraid."

Do not be afraid. Suffering doesn't mean that God doesn't love you. Trust in God's grace. Lean into that grace and you can get through any situation (Philippians 4:13).

God is going to put some situations in your path to help you grow in holiness and to help others experience His love. These situations might feel like chores some days. They might even feel like obstacles in your life from time to time. You can reject them and run from them. You can get through them with a bad attitude, or you can embrace them and trust in the Lord's plans.

Mary's love for the Father allowed her to fulfill her vocation with joy and with grace. It wasn't easy, but it wasn't a chore. The more you seek to love your Heavenly Father and to live a life like Mary's, the more fulfilling your life will become and the less you will feel like you're doing chores.

Life is only a chore if you let it be. Life can also be an adventure if you just "let it be...done according to God's will."

THE "LOAVES AND FISH" KID
THE BIBLE'S FIRST BUSBOY

AT AGE TEN, I decided I wanted to make some money. My allowance just wasn't cutting it. There were skateboard parts to buy and video games to master, so I told my parents I needed a higher allowance. They told me to get a job. Over the next few years I delivered thousands of newspapers. I delivered over 200 papers a day. Long before people got their news online, I was their search engine. I had a spotless record and a growing bank account. I took pride in my work. Once high school started, though, I had to find a different job, one that worked with my schedules for school, sports and band. I had tasted freedom with my own stream of income and I didn't want to live without it. I soon traded in newspapers for a spot-ridden apron and tray. I took a job as a lowly busboy in a nearby restaurant.

I never understood why they called the job "busboy." Later, though, I learned that the word "busboy" comes from the Latin word *omnibus*, which means "for all." It was applied to busboys because it is their job to do "anything and everything for anyone and everyone" in the restaurant. Truthfully, that's how it was.

I did everything. I set the tables, delivered food, cleared plates, restocked food, wiped down tables, swept and vacuumed. You name it; I did it. Customers didn't know my name. Customers didn't know how hard I was working behind the scenes or how badly I needed money, especially since I was saving for college. The only things that mattered to them were that their water glasses were always full, their baskets of chips were abundant, and the salsa endlessly flowed like a waterfall of spicy goodness. I was on the main stage every night, but somehow I remained almost anonymous and behind the scenes. People left that restaurant more stuffed than the enchiladas and gassier than an eighteen-wheeler. Each night, the waiters may have left with far more money in their pockets, but I fell into bed with the great satisfaction of knowing I had gone above and beyond the call of duty.

St. Martha is the patron saint of waiters and waitresses. You might remember how she waited on and served the Lord (Luke 10:38-42). However, there is no official patron saint designated specifically for busboys or busgirls, which got me to thinking. I'd like to suggest one character, in particular, who I think would make a great patron saint of busboys.

JESUS AND THE LUNCH RUSH

Jesus performed countless miracles during His time on earth. We are blessed that many of them were written down in the gospels. One of the miracles that appears in all four gospel accounts, and one of the most famous miracles of all time, is the multiplication of the loaves and the fish.

You have probably heard this story more times than you can count. Sometimes it's important to read it again, however, with your own eyes. Often times when you look at it on your own, rather than having others read it to you, you'll pick up on little details you might have missed in the past.

Read **John 6:1-14** and pay attention to the details.

Okay, now answer the following questions:

> *Where did this take place, next to what famous site?*
> *When did this take place, during what feast?*
> *How much money would still not be enough to feed everyone?*
> *Who tells Jesus about the boy with the food?*
> *How much food does the boy have?*
> *What kind of bread was it?*
> *How many men were there, not counting the women and children?*
> *What, specifically, did Jesus do with the bread and fish?*
> *How much food was left over after Jesus' miracle?*

Did you catch any details you had forgotten? Did you notice anything new?

Over the years, I've heard a lot of priests and speakers talk about "the boy with the loaves and the fish." They always praised his generosity and affirmed his sacrifice. While I don't want to disagree, because the boy does deserve our admiration, the homilies and talks always annoy me a little.

First, I have never liked the fact that the kid didn't have a name. I mean, of course *he had a name,* but the gospel writers don't tell us what it is, which bothers me. If this kid is so important, why didn't someone stop to get a name? I think we should call him **Eddie**. Eddie sounds like a good guy. Eddie's the kind of kid who'll share his lunch with you at school when you accidentally leave yours on the counter. Yep, I vote that from here on out, or at least in this book, we officially refer to "the loaves and fish kid" as Eddie.

> **The Sea of Galilee is approximately thirteen miles long and five miles wide. It is a very important site in the gospels.**

> **Twelve is a very symbolic number in the Bible. There were twelve Tribes of Israel and Christ chose twelve Apostles for this reason.**

Next, I don't like the fact that every speaker paints such a heroic picture of Eddie. We praise this boy because he turned over his lunch to a bunch of hungry-looking, grown men. I mean, think about it for a second. If you're a young guy and some big dudes (fishermen, no less) surround you and ask what's in your basket, you have two choices: one results in possibly getting beaten up, the other results in an unintentional fast for the remainder of the day. Eddie may not have been as courageous as he was smart. While we have no way of knowing, it is fun to think about, isn't it? Scripture should capture our imagination and cause us to think. When you're reading a story, don't just ask, "What is this saying *to me?*" Really put yourself into the

After Jesus' miracle with the loaves and fish, he goes on to explain a greater miracle with bread: the Eucharist (John 6:22-71).

scene, into each character's sandals and ask, "What is this saying *about me?*"

Eddie didn't set out to be a hero. We don't even know what he was doing there that day. Maybe he just noticed the crowd while walking by the Sea of Galilee and decided to investigate. Maybe, like David, he was just delivering lunch to someone in his family when he found himself in an awkward situation.

Barley was considered "poor peoples' food". Since the boy was not wealthy, his sacrifice is that much more powerful.

Possibly, the most important part of Eddie's story isn't what he did, but *why he did it.* What did he hear in the apostles' voices? What did he see in Jesus' eyes? He was most likely from a poor family. He probably fit right in with the masses of people who came to Jesus hungry. Only this day, for some reason, Eddie had some food. He didn't know what Christ was going to do, but he gave the Lord all that he had. Christ honored Eddie's sacrifice, blessings thousands of people through it.

The "loaves" were probably more the size of buns.

All Eddie did was give back to God what he had already been given. That food, while it was technically Eddie's, was really God's. Every gift you have is a gift from God. Everything you have, even those things you buy with your own money, is a gift from God. Eddie didn't withhold creation (loaves and fish) from his Creator and, as a result, even more of God's creation (literally thousands) was blessed by it.

Never underestimate how much God can do with a little. Never underestimate how much God can do with you, an ordinary person, on an ordinary day.

FINDING YOUR STORY IN "EDDIE'S" STORY

Have you ever given everything you had to the Lord?

Do you give your absolute best to everything you do?

Is it more desirable for you to be famous or to be faithful? To be rich or to be holy?

Do you think Eddie would care that his name isn't listed in the gospel accounts? Or do you think he was so overwhelmed with what he witnessed that *his glory* was the furthest thing from his mind?

He witnessed a miracle of love. He witnessed God in action. The God of the universe thought enough of Eddie to invite him to play a major role in one of the most famous and miraculous moments in history. He looked Love in the eyes and watched how Love magnified his little act of love. Eddie's life was instantly changed forever.

Just think about how many people benefited from Eddie's charity, and not just the thousands on the shore of the sea. Billions of souls have read and heard this true story, having their lives both challenged and blessed by it.

For a nameless kid, he made quite a name for himself. How about you?

Do you worry that your best just isn't good enough? You have more to offer than you think. When you give God your everything, He can do amazing things. God can do *miraculous things* with what you offer back to Him.

The first thing you have to do is remember where your gifts, talents and blessings come from. They are all gifts from God. When you put them back into His hands, for His use and for His glory, He can (and will) do incredible things – not only in your life, but also in the countless lives of other people. You are powerful beyond your wildest dreams. Did you know that? There is power in sacrifice. And, just as Jesus did with Eddie, God not only unleashes that power when you put your gifts in His hands, He multiplies them!

Pour your best into everything you do. Take pride in your schoolwork. Take responsibility around the house. Make your room the kind of place that would make your parents proud. Whatever it is that you like to do – sports, dance, music, writing – do it well. Give it your best, because the God who gave you that talent deserves your best at all times (Colossians 3:15-17).

You don't have to be all things to all people, but you're invited to be the absolute best version of yourself that you can be, every hour of the day. And you can do that by putting others first, by serving them just like Jesus did (John 13:15). If you live this way, you won't be bussing the banquet table in heaven. You'll be sitting as the guest of honor, right beside Jesus, enjoying the fruits of a job well done and a life well lived.

TIMOTHY
THE BIBLE'S LAST APPRENTICE

WHEN PEOPLE ASK you, "What are you going to be when you grow up?" how do you respond? What are your dreams for your future? Have they changed at all? Often times when we think about our future job, we try to envision ourselves in settings that we think would make us happy. At the same time, we also try to eliminate certain jobs based on things we dislike.

For example, if you dislike blood, you will probably cross doctor or paramedic off of your potential job list. If you have a fear of heights, you probably won't apply to be a skydiving instructor or a window washer. If you are terrible at math, you might want to avoid accounting. If you are a "germ-a-phobe," you probably won't enjoy plumbing. And if you lack patience, teaching is probably not for you.

Some people pick jobs for the power, others for the hours, and many for the money. Some people just take whatever they can get and wait until something better comes along. Work is work. There are bills to pay and food to buy. A job is a job, right?

Well, yes and no.

Where does God fit into all this? At what point do you stop and really pray to God, asking Him to guide you into your future, not only including your job, but also your vocation? Do you pray about whether you are called to be married or single, a priest or religious sister or brother?

Your parents might also have a plan for you. You might have the "perfect" plan for your own life. As well-intentioned and perfect as your plan or your parents' plans are, they are nowhere near as perfect as God's plan for you.

Read **Jeremiah 29:11-12**. Commit it to memory. It's one of the most important verses you can pray as you consider your future. God has a plan for your life, one that only you can fulfill. It begins with you trusting Him and saying yes.

St. Paul had a plan for his life. God had another.

St. Paul started out merely as Saul, a very intelligent and well-respected man, with a strong hatred for Christians. Saul changed his mind, however, after the Lord spoke to his heart. Saul went from despising those who followed Jesus to giving his very life so that everyone in the world would know of Christ's love. Saul became St. Paul; the world's greatest missionary and the writer of almost half of the New Testament. He didn't know where God was going to lead him from day to day, or from year to year. St. Paul was constantly praying, asking the Holy Spirit to guide and direct his path (Acts 16:6).

Timothy means "honored by God."

St. Paul met an array of interesting people on his travels around the Mediterranean world. Some were friendly. Many were not. During his first missionary journey, St. Paul, along with St. Barnabas, ended up in an area called Galatia, located in modern day Turkey. There, in the cities of Derbe and Lystra, they preached the gospel message in the marketplace each day. It was there that a young man named Timothy, probably a teenager, first heard the good news of Jesus Christ from his future mentor and friend, St. Paul.

Timothy's story picks up several years later. When St. Paul and his new traveling companion, Silas, come back through Galatia on another missionary journey, a now young adult Timothy catches their attention.

TINY TIM GROWS INTO ST. TIMOTHY

The Acts of the Apostles tells us that Timothy was the son of a Jewish mother and a Greek father. He must have learned about the faith and about the Hebrew Scriptures from his mother, Lois, and his grandmother, Eunice (2 Tim. 1:5). He was apparently a very well-respected young man in his community, and the leaders there spoke so highly of him that St. Paul invited Timothy along on his missionary work (Acts 16:1-2).

Timothy was likely born in Lystra (modern day Turkey).

The rest of what we know about St. Timothy we learn from the rest of St. Paul's letters, which are called *epistles*. Over the next fifteen to twenty years, St. Timothy would see a whole new world. God sent Timothy into situations the young disciple never would have chosen on his own.

Timothy traveled with Paul to Philippi and began to watch over the newly formed Church there. Later, Timothy would travel to Thessalonica, preaching and teaching the Gospel. Timothy was with Paul as he wrote his letters to the good people of Thessalonica (1 & 2 Thessalonians), traveled to Ephesus and back through Greece. In addition to other travels, Timothy would be with Paul during his imprisonment in Rome and, eventually, be left in Ephesus as a leader, to deal with problems that were erupting there (2 Timothy 1:4).

St. Paul commends Timothy for his loyalty in Phil. 2:19.

There are two letters to Timothy in the New Testament and both are attributed to St. Paul. When you read them, you can see the love and friendship that the two great evangelists shared. St. Paul respected St. Timothy very much and spoke highly of him (Phil. 2:19-22).

Timothy boldly confronted false teachers (1 Tim. 1:3).

Timothy must have been feeling overwhelmed by his position in Ephesus. It's tough enough being a young leader, teaching about God and His Word to people twice your age. St. Paul's letters are written to strengthen and encourage St. Timothy. There were many false teachers and inappropriate practices going on in Ephesus, which were challenging for St. Timothy.

Take a few minutes and read **1 Timothy 4:6-16** and **2 Timothy 4:1-6**.

1 Timothy 4:12 is one of the most famous "teen" verses in the Bible.

In St. Paul, Timothy had more than a good friend or traveling companion. St. Paul was Timothy's mentor and teacher. This makes St. Timothy one of the Bible's last known apprentices, and a true gift to the early Church. Tradition tells us that St. Timothy continued ministering in Ephesus and was eventually martyred for the faith under the Emperor Domitian (sometime between A.D. 81-96).

Growing up in Lystra, St. Timothy probably had different plans for his life. No young boy's dream is to be chased out of towns, mocked and eventually martyred for the faith. At the same time, St. Timothy also knew a deeper joy that many never experience: the joy of knowing Jesus Christ intimately and sharing in His life and grace on a daily basis. St. Timothy saw the world. St. Timothy witnessed miracles. St. Timothy humbly spoke with authority and power as he served Jesus Christ and His Church. Through St. Timothy's "yes" to God, countless souls came to know God and were saved. Today, over 2000 years later, we honor St. Timothy as one of the great early saints of our Church.

FINDING YOUR STORY IN TIMOTHY'S STORY

Are you willing to do what God calls you to do and to go where God calls you to go?

Are you open to whatever vocation, even priesthood or religious life, that God calls you to?

Are you willing to be uncomfortable or to suffer for your faith?

Do you doubt yourself? Do you doubt God's presence within you?

You are a work of art, unique and beautiful and amazing. You are a complete, one-of-a-kind masterpiece, created and handcrafted by a creative Creator. You are designed to reflect the light of Christ to all whom you encounter.

These are all true statements, whether or not you agree with them. Do you believe these statements? Do you feel this way about yourself? Do you feel unique and beautiful? Do you believe you are the handiwork of God, created and designed with purpose and dignity? Do you believe you glorify Him and reflect His light to the world?

If not, it might be time to head to the Sacrament of Reconciliation and get rid of the blinders we call sin. If not, it might be a sign that you need to pray more, to read more Sacred Scripture, and to start seeing yourself as God sees you, rather than how you have begun to see yourself.

Read and pray these Scripture passages:

- Psalm 139:14-16
- Matthew 10:30
- Ephesians 2:10
- Genesis 1:26-27
- Isaiah 41:10

God believes in you so strongly that He doesn't leave you alone. God sends you people in your life to offer you good examples. Hopefully, they're in your own home. Hopefully, there are holy and joyful people in your parish and your school. God will send you who you need just as He did for Timothy.

Timothy's mother taught him the Jewish faith where his father, a Greek, could not. God didn't leave Timothy spiritually orphaned, though. He sent him St. Paul to be his mentor, guide, and spiritual foster father. God provided for young Timothy so he could fulfill the role and vocation that God had designed for him. God will do the same for you. God believes in you more than you believe in yourself.

Live like Timothy. Be open. Stay humble. Follow holy people. Ask questions. Keep learning. Be courageous. Never stop praying. Live. Love.

St. Timothy knew how to love people and it is love, not just knowledge of the faith, that wins hearts for Jesus Christ. If the person you are talking to doesn't believe that you love them, it doesn't matter how smart you are when you speak to them. Love changes lives. Love heals wounds. Love saves souls.

God believes in you. I believe in you, too.

The question is not whether or not God will send you a mentor. God will send people, holy people, to lead you. The question is: will you follow?

ADDITIONAL
RESOURCES

THE CATHOLIC TEEN BIBLE

Want to offer teens a Bible that takes them deeper into Scripture? The Catholic Teen Bible from Life Teen meets teenagers where they are in their faith walk with authentic, clear and candid language. With 128 supplemental pages of distinctively Catholic resources, this Bible helps teens grow in their love for the Sacred Scriptures and introduces them to God's plan for their lives as revealed in His Sacred Word.

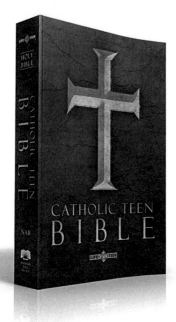

FEATURES
- 128 pages of full-color original content from Life Teen, 64 pages in the front and 64 pages in the back leaving the Biblical text, itself, undisturbed
- An overview of all 73 books of the Bible
- Sections on how to read Scripture – what to watch for and "watch out" for
- Lists of important events, cross-referenced with Scripture verses
- A thematic concordance with over 600 verses
- An overview of the Covenants in Scripture and their significance
- A Glossary of Biblical terms
- Quotes from the Saints on Scripture
- Contains dozens of photos of classic works of Christian art
- Imprimatur by Bishop

A DISTINCTLY CATHOLIC RESOURCE:
- Tradition and Scripture explained
- A guide to the Rosary and Scriptures for all 20 decades
- The Biblical basis for all seven Sacraments of the Roman Catholic Church
- Practical apologetics - verses to help explain the faith
- Relating Scripture and the Mass - a list of Scripture verses from the Mass
- A guide to Lectio Divina – teaching teens how to pray the Scriptures
- The full cycle of Sunday readings

*Paperback, 5.25"x8", 1437 pages, **$22.95***

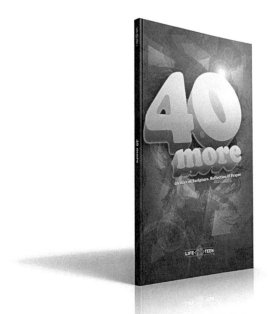

40 MORE
40 DAYS OF SCRIPTURE,
REFLECTION AND PRAYER

What if you gave God 40 days to deepen your relationship with Him? Just 40 days out of your life, in which you committed to reading and praying Scripture just ten minutes a day. If you've ever said to yourself, "I need to pray more" or "I need to start reading the Bible more," this book is for you.

This book is a challenge for you to make a commitment to daily prayer over 40 days. For each day there is a Scripture passage, questions, reflection and prayer. You can use it during Lent, Easter Season, as a follow up to a retreat or simply in Ordinary Time. *40 More* is not just a daily devotional, but also a tool to help form a life-long habit of prayer. Useful for all ages, but especially great for teenagers.

Paperback, 5.5"x8.5", 106 pages, $9.95

SWORD
OF THE SPIRIT

by Christopher Cuddy & Mark Hart
Foreword by Scott Hahn

Few Christians in history have had the impact on the Church that St. Paul did. Unfortunately, though, his theology is so deep and his writings are so intricate that many modern Catholics don't know where to begin.

Written in concise and practical language, *Sword of the Spirit: A Beginners Guide to St. Paul,* offers the reader, a clear understanding of Catholic doctrine as outlined and exemplified through St. Paul's epistles, in particular his Letter to the Romans. Each chapter is cross-referenced with Scripture and Catechism references, essential footnotes and advice based upon the writings of St. Paul. Get a glimpse into the mind and heart of this great saint! Encounter the love that inspired him to travel thousands of miles over dozens of years all for the sake of Christ and His Kingdom. This book is great for teens or adults.

*Discussion questions for book groups are available, too, for free download at www.catholicyouthministry.com.

*Paperback, 5.5"x8.5", 190 pages, **$14.95***

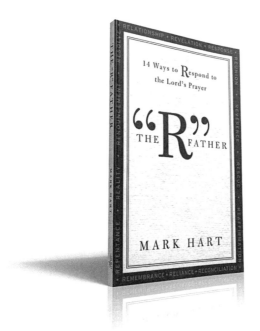

THE "R" FATHER

The Lord's Prayer is so familiar to us that we risk reciting it, not praying it. Life Teen Executive Vice President, Mark Hart says that the Our Father is an invitation into a daily relationship with God and suggests 14 ways we can respond to him in this prayer. All begin with the letter "R"—from "remembrance" and "repentance" to "reliance" and "resolve." Hart's engaging style will appeal to Catholics both young and old, while his insights will help readers gain a deeper understanding of the love that our Father pours out on us.

"Handle this book with prayer. It may shatter your childish notions about God, even as it makes you more childlike in the presence of your heavenly Father. This can be the first step in a loving relationship that grows stronger forever." – Dr. Scott Hahn, Franciscan University of Steubenville

Paperback, 5.25"x 8", 183 pages, **$11.95**

SUNDAY, SUNDAY, SUNDAY PODCAST

The Bible Geek®, Mark Hart, prepares you for the upcoming Sunday Catholic Mass readings. Don't show up to Mass unprepared! Pray through the readings, listen to this podcast, pay attention at Mass, and get ready to grow that much closer to Christ. The Sunday Sunday Sunday podcast is brought to you by your friends at LifeTeen.com.

You can listen online at www.lifeteen.com or find all of our podcasts on iTunes by searching "lifeteen.com".

T3:
THE TEEN TIMELINE

The Teen Timeline—or *T3*—is the teen version of the revolutionary Great Adventure Bible Timeline learning system that hundreds of thousands of Catholic adults have used to learn the Bible. Life Teen Executive Vice President, Mark Hart, makes the Bible come alive for Catholic teens by unpacking God's Word in a way they can relate to. *T3* teaches teens the Bible by showing them the "big picture" of salvation history. When young students of the Bible first understand the "story," they are eager to learn more. The net result: teens begin to wrap their minds and hearts around the Scriptures. They come to see the Bible as a relevant part of their lives.

- 8 Part DVD Series: **$99.95**
- 8 Part Audio CD Series: **$39.95**
- Leader's Manual: **$19.95**
- Study Kit: **$19.95**

T3: MATTHEW
THY KINGDOM COME

Created and hosted by Life Teen Executive Vice President, Mark Hart, *Thy Kingdom Come* picks up where *T3* left off, as Mark takes your teens on an in-depth journey into the heart of God. Follow along as the group encounters the authentic Jesus of the gospels. Enter into the drama of Christ's family tree, the birth of our Savior, His duel in the desert with Satan, and the life-changing truths of His Sermon on the Mount. Experience Jesus' ministry unfold through His miracles and parables. Be there as our Lord triumphantly enters into Jerusalem on His way to the cross, tomb, and resurrection. Your teens will feel like they are walking along with the apostles, as they learn about the inception of the Catholic Church, the papacy, and the Sacraments, firsthand.

- 8 Part DVD Series: **$99.95**
- 8 Part Audio CD Series: **$39.95**
- Leader's Manual: **$18.95**
- Study Kit: **$9.95**

To order call **1-800-809-3902** or visit **www.lifeteen.com/store**

T3: ACTS
THE KEYS AND THE SWORD

T3: Acts–The Keys and the Sword equips teens with a foundational understanding of the main characters, doctrines, events, and journeys that make up this incredible "gospel of the Holy Spirit." Beginning with the Ascension and Pentecost, these four sessions offer a deeper look at Sts. Peter and Paul, the evolution of the early Christian Church, the call to evangelization, the sacramental ministry, the first Christian communities, the trials of an evangelist, the call to offer our lives as a living witness, and much more. *T3: Acts* hosted by Life Teen Executive Vice President, Mark Hart, will leave your young people laughing, engaged, and ready for more!

- 2 Part DVD Series: **$49.95**
- 2 Part Audio CD Series: **$24.95**
- Student Workbook: **$7.95**
- Leader's Guide: **$14.95**

T3: REVELATION
THE LION AND THE LAMB

In *T3:Revelation–The Lion and the Lamb*, Mark Hart calms the concerns and unpacks the myths about Revelation, the end times, the mark of the beast, and so much more. *T3:Revelation* gives your teens an invaluable foundation for understanding the book of Revelation, while pointing out its modern significance, practical application, and daily relevance to a teenager's life. In each of the four lessons, Mark skillfully unpacks the book's main points and key chapters, while continually referring to the wisdom offered by our Catholic faith.

- 2 Part DVD Series: **$49.95**
- 2 Part Audio CD Series: **$24.95**
- Student Workbook: **$7.95**
- Leader's Guide: **$14.95**